All The Words That Heal Me

Cherish Muzik

Tradepaper ISBN: 979-8-9881517-1-5

Hardback ISBN: 979-8-9881517-2-2

E-book ISBN:979-8-9881517-0-8

Dedicated to Xavier, Cedric, and Symphony

for inspiring me to trust my heart and heal.

To Nathaniel for always and forever being in my corner.

I love you all.

Preface

Healing doesn't happen without making friends with the pain.

It requires us to date our darkness so we may fall in love with the illusions that separated us from our divinity. And yes, I said "fall in love" because love is the energy of alchemy and healing.

This doesn't mean that I love the trauma that hurt me. However, it does mean that I learn to love myself and all parts of who I am, including the parts of me that have experienced trauma. Too often we cut ourselves off from our pain. We deny it. Numb it. Mask it. But it never goes away on its own, because our pain is waiting for *us* to integrate it and learn from it from a place of love and grace. Until we learn how to bring all the pieces of our soul puzzle together, we will always feel fragmented, like something is missing. That fragmentation is why we look to other people to make us whole or form addictions to make us forget our pain.

But the pain is the prodigal parts of us longing to come home to our heart...

The god we are taught to fear is a god that created outcasts damned to hell. So it's no wonder we cast parts of our lives, ourselves, to proverbial hell—even if we are religious. Just look at how our society treats those who make mistakes or lose their way.

But this is the way of hiding pain, covering it up, but not healing it.

Until the pain is loved and understood, we create illusions that repeat patterns of pain.

The illusion of not being chosen or not-enoughness. Stories we tell ourselves to justify why it was acceptable to be treated as if we didn't matter. Stories of lack or scarcity made us create stories or situations where we had to steal, lie, or cheat to get what we wanted or needed.

We don't want to be cast aside, so of course, we lied or allowed ourselves to be treated as less than. We didn't believe we deserved better.

The anger and the pain that brewed in the depths of our beings when someone reflected back to us the illusions, we carried surfaced as deep rage. How dare they!

We trusted them.

We believed them.

But deep down inside, we knew better. We wanted to prove ourselves right, even if right meant making ourselves victims of betrayal. We looked to someone else to save us from the story that we weren't enough, only to discover that they just reinforced a story we believed about ourselves.

They broke promises we knew they couldn't keep.

But we thought we were different.

We thought we were special.

We were wrong.

How dare they make us wrong!

Yet, we knew it.

Our wholeness comes from within.

To look to someone or something outside of us to validate us is a recipe for disaster.

This is when shit falls apart.

This is where the healing begins. The truth has been revealed. Do we continue to force our illusion, stuffing the truth into the corner of our closets and hoping we can pile more lies and denials on top? Or do we lovingly examine the contents of our emotional closets so we can clean out the stink of our self-depreciation?

Denial is how we got here. Eventually, the truth wins and wants out. The truth will always move to the light and will expose all that contradicts it. The truth is love and only love is real.

Everything that is not love is an illusion. The truth sweeps through the closet and clears out every lie we told ourselves to keep our illusions intact.

Everything falls apart so we may sort the truth from the lies.

And when we sort this all out, we discover how we participated in our own pain. *Or we don't do the healing and sorting, and we repeat the cycle over and over again until we don't or until we die.*

But when we decided enough is enough and face ourselves, then anger, shame, depression, and grief come to the room to be heard. *We can't ignore these feelings. They need to be a part of the conversation about healing, because these are the ignored parts of us that got us into this situation to begin with.*

Happiness comes from working through negative emotions and dismantling the hold those stories have on our souls. Those stories come from trauma—misguided, scarcity, or fear-based programming. But when we ignore the calls to heal and go straight to relationships because of a desperation to be happy, we choose people and situations who will in fact make us feel terribly unhappy, even shitty. These relationships are essentially trauma bonds we mistake for love we hoped would rescue us from our pain. Maybe there will be sparks of the possibility of happiness, but they are never rooted in authenticity. They are just a temporary distraction from our pain illusions.

We will go round and round in cycles of pain with someone or some "thing," trying to get to happiness from it, only to end up in the same place as we were before ... sometimes worse. We have to get off the merry-go-round, heal, and change. We can't get happiness from anyone or anything until we have that foundation independent of circumstances.

To avoid this step destines us to repeat it. We can change partners or environments, but if we don't do the inner work, we get the same results.

*Wherever we go, there we are ... After a while, we need to realize the truth ... The pattern of unhappiness is rooted within **us** ... We keep choosing people or situations that reinforce that pattern. To break the pattern, we have to get to the root and honor what we find there ... Chances are it won't be pretty, but it's divine and necessary.*

The anger, the sadness, the jealousy, the hatred, all the things we try to mask or pretend away, are feelings of love trapped behind the idea that we aren't deserving of love. It's like the negative emotions are the ground we must break and dig through to get the secret treasure. The dirt as the pattern has a purpose as it protected us at one time, but soon it became a burden that prevented us from the one thing we desired: love.

"Dirt and dust" that cover our treasure are the limiting beliefs we carry. The dirt is the story or person we are told to let go of because "it no longer serves us." This dirt must be cleared away.

When shit falls apart, we are being called to go beneath the rubble and clean house. We go through the mess and grieve the versions of us that "held on to and put up with" things that contradict our desire for love and peace. We falsely believed our ticket to happiness was in those things or people.

When we discover how wrong we were ... how wrong they were ... anger and grief surface ... These emotions are necessary portals we must travel through to align with self-love and peace.

The Words That Hurt

This Is The Container

This is an evolution of me.

My painful parts that grew into a field of healing.

I needed somewhere to put these words so that the horrors couldn't take up permanency in my cells.

Generations

Nothing is forever

I could have let the pain eat me alive

So when I died I would finally taste freedom.

That's what my mother did.

I'm not my mother.

I refuse to be my mother.

But I see her smile in me.

Her green eyes became my brown.

I am her

The alternate version

The her she always wanted to be

And pushed me to be

Which meant I had to confront her pain

To heal myself from mine

Because the only reason I had it

Was because she denied it

Wouldn't deal with it

Numbed it

So I had to nurture her

And nurture me

I told her she could make it through this

She told me

"I'm not like you"

But you are because you made me

Funny I heard myself tell my daughter the other day

"I'm not like you"

But I am, just more worn around the edges

The me I wanted to be

Without the heaviness of trauma

I absorbed so much to keep it from passing on

Still some slipped through and I feel like a failure ...

She takes off with the wind

Never worrying where she will land

She always has a safe place to land

I took off with the wind too,

But nowhere was safe

I feared landing

I just wanted an escape

There is no escaping though

Even with all the vodka my mom couldn't escape

And that's why I'm not her

While also being her

I escaped differently

Then I caught myself where she couldn't

I'm her without fear

My daughter is me without the fear

May this healing train of fearlessness

Continue through generations

So we evolve into our original Goddess form.

How Bad Do You Want It?

Have you ever needed something to work so bad that you compromised all your goodness to see it through because you didn't want all that you put into it to be a waste of time? Well ...

Don't.

Let it go.

No one or no thing is worth compromising your essence for.

If you end it now, before you die, even if you only have days left to live, then no time was wasted.

You took a chance and tasted living before dying.

Room

It's not that I didn't love you
it's that loving you meant
there was nothing left for me.

Narcissist

Nothing about you interests me
Only the memory of who I thought was
A man
Who was capable of loving
In the deepest way I loved
No
You are anything but
Just the illusion of a human who cared
And bombed me into believing that I was the one
But you did the same thing to her, and her, and her
And her, and her, and her as well ...
A man who creates illusions with everyone
Is not a man
But a trickster disguised
With no soul
Draining life
For its selfish existence

Remember

Remember when I came to you to love me
and you said no?
Remember when you spoke hurtful words
and I cried?
Remember when I asked
and you denied?
You remember
and so do I
Now you want me to forget
You ask me,
How could you?
But don't you remember?
I already gave myself to you
Now we're just a contract
And soon the contract will end
But you don't know it yet
guilt
pain
lies
love
forgive
and I can't forget

You put me out there

You pushed me away

You weren't interested

Then you twisted it

You twisted me

To fit your story

You held on

For your benefit

Selfish

you just…

OK ... this sucks.

Loving you isn't all it's cracked up to be.

Not today.

Today is one of those days I am reminded that our timing is
off

There's nothing really for us to hold on to.

What are you doing?

Don't you think of calling me first thing in the morning like
I do?

If you don't,

Then why am I still here? Why am I still doing this?

How do I explain my lack of love for me?

If I allow myself to be ignored or put off, knowing my
needs are not being met, then why am I bothering?

Plenty of men want me.

Plenty of them call, text, and email me daily, hourly, just
because they are thinking of mc.

They want to be first.

But you don't

you just ...

Choices

I've been here before
Between love that never was
And love that "kinda" is
Kinda is better than nothing
Right?
You said it's better to feel pain
Then put others through it
But this pain trickles down
To those others,
And I still love you
But you're pulling away
Forcing me to love
In the "kinda" way
That makes sense to everyone else
Yet leaves me alone in my thoughts
Of you
When I fall asleep
Can we make a different choice now
Everything has changed
Except for this love that never was
Let's make it a love that *is*
And set ourselves free from this "kinda" love

For true love

Last Night

I know you love me, but I'm not going to text you first.

You dropped over the edge with me last night.

We ravaged and savored each moment of our fall together. There's no way I went to that place alone.

You were there, too.

Even though you aren't used to admitting it.

You want me.

It consumed you as I drank you last night.

I'm in your head.

Don't fight it.

Loving me is not a weakness because it's my love that makes you strong.

It's why you keep coming back.

Just drop all your weapons of mass protection and love me back.

Say it.

I will set you free.

In the beginning

I loved you

Then ...

Sand In The Hourglass

Moving through time
passing days
nights go by
and I'm still loving you
Moving through time
hours slow
minutes tick on
and I'm still wanting you
Time
Such a painful reminder
what is
what isn't
what could be
what was
Do you hear my voice in your ears?
Do you feel my touch on your skin'?
Is this all so maddening to you
like it is for me?
How are we supposed to do this?
How have we done it?
Ten years or more have gone by
and we are still in love

but never together

just wishing we could be

and if I wanted this torture to end

could I make it stop?

Never

I can't stop loving you

My heart has no choice in this matter

It is what it is

that's your take

brutally honest

painfully true

Our love is and forever will be

Like it or not

Her

I fell in love with you when I was young and unknowing

I'm still young

I'm still unknowing

My stomach feels pain

Heart is torn

I repeat to myself

"We have a family"

"We have a family"

And

"I don't want to be like her"

"I don't want to be like her"

My mother.

Whatever I do,

I swear

I will never be like her.

But,

If not her, then who?

I don't know.

Stepping forward into blindness,

I tell you,

I love you, but

But what?

Your words hurt me.

Why do your words hurt so much?

It's because I love you

But

You keep hurting me

Then you say

Get over it.

I can't

I can't because I don't want to be like her.

I love you, but

I love myself more.

What Time Is It?

Timing.

Often we miss so many chances at relationships or opportunities because of timing or our failure to act when the opportunity arises. Usually, we just ignore it, deny it, or not believe in it ... Then it goes away, and we realize we've missed something. Then we spend the next however many years trying to get the chance again

Edit: time isn't real and I've lost nothing in figuring it out. What's meant for me will be there for me infinitely.

Feeling It

A blessing to feel

All the feelings

To be in touch with you

To understand

To get it

It comes easy

Too easy

I want to shut it off

But I can't

Not without drugs

Or some other

Self-destructive habit

That would make no sense

To do now

because

I already know

It won't work

Just gotta feel them

The Exorcism

Last night I decided, any habitual memory of you, any moment of weakness where I felt the need to reach out to you, needed to be exorcised from my physical and spiritual body. There was never an authentic connection between us. You are a leech, a parasitic spirit, that preys upon loving souls. Your main purpose is to suck the love from them to fill all your dark spaces with their light. In order to gain our empathy, you come to us broken, tired, hurting ... and because we are kind souls, empathetic souls unaware of boundaries, we open the window for the vampire to come in.

Entanglement

How do you untangle three cords that decided to tangle at conception?

You don't

Their souls know the story

But the bodies don't

So they resist

They judge

They depend

Until one wakes up and sees

This is exactly how it's supposed to be

To evolve and expand

Is this it?

In the hollows of my mind,

I quietly sit and wonder,

Is this it?

My life is good.

My baby is healthy.

We have food over our heads

And a roof in our bellies.

Most of the bills are paid

On time, but not always.

You don't smile like before.

It seems like being with me

Hurts you.

Not because I'm a bitch,

But just being who I am bothers you.

I want you to love me

The way to your heart escapes me.

"This is it," you yell.

"There's nothing more," you mumble.

"Your expectations are too high," you sigh.

It's not enough for me, I cry.

I need to feel you and I can't.

I'm dying a slow death starting at twenty-three,

Can I make it to thirty? Forty?

Can I live like this for the rest of my life?

No, I whisper.

I can't

I won't

This can't be it.

Maybe for you but not for me.

This isn't it.

I can't stop loving you

My heart has no choice in this matter

It is what it is

that's your take

brutally honest

painfully true

Trauma Bond

Addiction to drama disguised

I was the love

It was never you

You reflected the love that was me

But that love was never in you

It was me

And I couldn't see

No matter how much I wanted to believe

The lies that dripped from your lips

I was hypnotized by desperation

To be seen

Felt

Received

By a special soul

You pretended to be

But that soul was me

Mine

What I wanted from you

Was in me

And the more I tried to get you to see me

The more my heart broke for me

To love me

Heal me

Receive me

Feel me

And believe me

The day I saw you for who you really are

I can back to me

And you became the symbol

Of the pain I used to keep love away

So thank you for playing the part

For being the demon I needed to see

To rescue me from me.

Beautiful Mess

Sometimes we have to shit all over ourselves and others ...
get it out of our system before we can get our shit together.
Not the easiest path, but nothing is easy.

Wrong or right

Shit happens

When we heal we hurt less

And we hurt others less

So heal

No Exceptions

You told me I was different.

I was the exception.

But the exception to what?

I was the one you dumped your secrets on.

Then one you left to frolic with another that made you lighter because I was carrying the weight of your darkness.

That's not different.

That's just dumb.

Not in a shaming way but in an "at what point did I forget my worth to put myself in this position of your shadow keeper" kind of way.

You choked me with your darkness and it turned you on to watch me gasp for breath beneath your hold on me . . . my ego said, "But we are different."

My soul said no, *we're just the one willing to trade our spirit for a chance to feel chosen. Choose yourself instead.*

Then your secrets came out, you twisted them to attract another sad soul, and off you go again lighter, and now her heart is heavy with wondering

how did I get here?

There are no exceptions

Just the ones who don't love themselves enough

Protector

I wonder if one of the reasons I felt the need to protect the women you were abusing was because the woman I needed to protect me didn't.

She didn't even protect herself.

So it was up to me to shield us both.

Then moving forward, too many of my friends and your lovers needed saving.

It wasn't my place to step onto the path of another soul.

But I wanted to warn them ...

I shined a light on the town spirit rapist though.

If they continued in the shadows, it was on them.

My mom avoided her light

Of speaking the truth

And it killed it her.

—*he's not worth it*

I Chose Me

I wasn't the one to sacrifice my soul to force you into commitment.

I wasn't the type to trap you with pregnancy, threats, or guilt.

I wasn't willing to throw it all away to give you the satisfaction of triangulated drama.

I was the one to walk away.

Move far away.

And every day you'd miss me and wish I was the one.

It was a choice between me and you.

I chose me.

I saw how you acted when the others laid their lives down for you.

You drained their life force and left them for dead.

I hope they recover and understand why I had to warn them.

Sour Juice

Go get yourself an orange if you want orange juice.

These lemons won't give you lemonade unless you're adding your *own* sugar and your *own* water.

He will say thanks, drink you depleted, and then leave you with an empty cup.

Flags

The first red flag I overlooked was how easily lies rolled off your tongue. Then next red flag was how you manipulated me to keep everything we did a secret. You told me it would destroy you. I loved you so destroying felt like death. Instead, I carried the weight of the betrayal I thought was my twin flame. I gained thirty pounds carrying your weakness of the spirit. You come off as the master of strength, but like everything else that is you, it's only on the surface. It was all too familiar, but it felt like the greatest love. I also loved my grandfather and kept his secrets, too. Until I didn't. You punished me for telling the truth and manipulated others to keep yourself safe. Trauma bonds are so fucking sneaky. Who knew my deepest pain would mask itself as my greatest love? My greatest love was me though ... not you. You were just a stop on the path back to my soul.

New Growth

You're the one I need to let go of the most.

The one who has caused the most hurt.

The most disruption.

But in that, you brought the biggest healing and the brightest awareness of who I am at the soul level.

My resentment toward you, toward the situation, is causing more harm than good.

I so badly wanted you to pay for everything you did.

At the same time, I've had to pay as well.

So my healing has come down to letting go of the story of pain and allowing the freedom to trickle in after it.

You were the fire that burned the earth of my soul.

You burned away all the weeds that grew from trauma. Then I cried.

I sobbed.

And my tears watered my earth and new growth emerged without you but also because of you.

Thank you for clearing the path so I could find my way back to my soul.

Stoicism

Stoicism, "to ensure hardship without a display of feelings and without complaint," is foundational to the oppressive systems of colonialism.

It's denial of emotions and the heart masked by the moral superiority of rightness.

Stoicism is not something to strive for, but rather something to free yourself from.

A stoic person is an unfeeling person.

A person who doesn't honor their own feelings will not honor others. That person isn't to be trusted with the heart. Stoic is a nice way to say sociopathic.

Like a workaholic is honorable because they can produce so much, yet work is still an addiction and it's equally destructive.

Stoicism encourages us to stuff our feelings down and pretend to be nice.

To have a good reputation even though the character is shit.

And who wants the inauthenticity of niceness draining their energy?

It's robotic. It's dry and rigid. It's lifeless. It's death while breathing.

Stoicism drips with a fear of truth and vulnerability.

Align

I'm aligning
letting go
loving unconditionally to magnetize my frequency
you're working hard
controlling everything
manipulating to get what you want.
We are not the same.

Love Lets Go

if you are afraid of trusting and letting go because you fear what you love will be lost

then

they're not worth holding onto.

the only way you know the love is real is by letting go.

Who's The Real Bad Guy Here?

I bet you didn't know that when you preyed on me you had met your match.

Look at us now.

Fighting in our heads even though we don't speak.

If I don't fight you, I miss you.

And I fight you because I miss you.

I'm inside out when it comes to you.

You are a stranger to me now.

What am I even doing writing about you?

I guess I still need a villain for my stories.

I can't be my own bad guy.

Vampires

You did this thing where you'd rest your head on my back when you found refuge inside me.

You were vulnerable then and I thought that was who you were always going to be with me.

You thought my juices were flowing from pleasure.

Instead, it was my blood oozing from the wounds

From you breaking my heart.

Energy vampires show no mercy.

You made that perfectly clear.

The Space Between Us

I remember the crisp air piercing between the few gaps where our skin wasn't touching.

It was a quiet reminder that you didn't completely fall into the depths of my soul.

But most of you did and for weeks I'd have to pry you off me so I could feel the oxygen in my lungs only to return to the night where I couldn't tell the difference between my tongue and your lips.

God's Grace

It's by grace we are not together.

We ignited darkness inside the pores of one another's skin
When we touched

That is why it felt so good to break one another into
Fractional pieces of scattered pleasure.

The problem was that is how we left one another.

Broken.

We sucked at putting one another back together.

Now I understand

Only I could repair myself.

But you made it almost impossible for me to stay intact.

That's why she is better off with you.

Her life's work is keeping you together in hopes that you
stay with her forever.

Maybe you will

But it will cost her

I knew better than that.

Cutting Cords

When I moved, I blocked you.

Then you bypassed my block and called me.

"Are you trying to block me?"

I said no. I don't know why I said no.

Yes, I was trying to block you to get my life back.

And your answer was ...

"You can never cut the cord of who we are to one another."

Then I performed a cord-cutting ceremony to set us both free.

Coward

You tried so desperately to destroy my family when in reality you made it stronger.

Thank you.

The best part of it all is l live for the truth and the truth scares the shit out of you.

My presence scares you.

I know the truth.

Coward.

Bitter Taste

Bitterness doesn't even begin to describe the stench of you
I tasted in my mouth when I said your name.

How can something I loved feel so disturbing on my
tongue? But I still had to speak about you.

I still had to speak your name to desensitize myself.

To taste the pain so my body could release your poison.

Why Women Need To Believe Women

Men don't believe women because

there are wives/girlfriends blaming women who got
involved with their boyfriends/husbands

because they were manipulated to believe your man's
words when he told them that you didn't exist or matter

Just like you believed him when he told you the other
women wouldn't leave him alone.

He played you both, but you blame the other women.

That's where you fucked up.

Believe her when she tells you the truth.

Believe your truth, not his.

No Winners

Dear victim that came after me ...

You didn't win.

He hasn't changed.

Stop believing him if you want to stop slowly destroying yourself.

Signed, the one who came before you and the victims before me and the ones who are involved now,

who know about you, but you don't know about them.

The Lie That Is You

The explosive fury that seared through my veins could have decimated entire civilizations

when

I realized the lie that was you.

But that would have also destroyed me.

So I clung to my own civility as best as I could ...

because my nonreaction was the most damaging to you.

I wonder if you hold a record for lies told so you could save your ass.

My Love is Liberation

The differences between me and the others are

I didn't manipulate you to be with me.

I didn't cling to you or claim you to make you stay.

Love isn't ownership.

How colonial of her.

My love was liberation and you chose bondage.

Backstory

You kept telling me that she didn't matter

But when I saw her social media, she clearly mattered

And when I asked you, you told me she was delusional

But am I delusional for believing you?

She thought I was "stalking"

I'm trying to reconcile the truth because everything felt like

Denial

My denial, hers, yours ...

Only to find out there were even more secrets!

She or they can have you.

You're not that great.

Great people don't go to the lengths that you did to cover their tracks.

My tracks were clear.

I wasn't lying to people in my world.

I put all my truth out in the open so I could see what aligned and what didn't.

You don't align.

I don't need to save face or prove my love to keep you.

I'm not a minion.

She is though.

Good luck with that.

Make It Make Sense

I'm embarrassed to admit that ...

I checked your social media feed

Ugh, I don't even like you.

But I'm looking for something ...

Trying to see the ridiculousness of it all

Make it make sense.

How can one lie so effortlessly?

And so many believe the story ...

That you and I both know isn't true?

You Started This

I'll never forget that it was you that pursued me.

You initiated the betrayal and I was so desperate for love
and attention

I jumped at the opportunity, blind to what was happening.

And I tried to end it 100 times.

On the 101st time, my heart was barely beating after being
broken all the times before.

My soul said this has to end or it will kill you.

I'll be damned if I let you suck the literal life out of me
nearly destroying everything else.

In order to shock my heart back into life

I had to make a heroic effort to save your next victim

only to realize it was too late.

She already believed you more than she believed herself.

So Wrong

I think what hurts me the most is

I was wrong about you.

I was wrong about how you felt about me.

I was wrong about how I reacted when I realized nothing about anything you ever did or said was remotely real or honest,

but I believed you.

I gave you my heart because I believed you.

I allowed you in between my thighs and I cried I love you because I believed you when you told me first.

I turned my life upside down because I believed you. Believing you was wrong and everyone told me not to trust you.

But I did.

And it hurts me that you betrayed my trust,

but what hurts me more is I deceived myself, my family, and my friends when I believed you.

And your response was to lie to me and deceive more.

I'm Not For You

You did your research

You stalked

You observed

You preyed

And you discovered that I can not be destroyed

I'm not for the weak

I'm not for you

Sometimes

Sometimes I'm the toxic one

I'm the one causing chaos

The one creating drama

Sometimes it was me

And I blamed you

I just didn't realize it was me at the time.

I really thought I was the victim

But that's the problem.

I thought I was the victim and that's exactly what I manifested—a situation where you'd hurt me.

My reactions to your actions ensured my victimization where I could say you hurt me ... but I was also choosing it unconsciously ... then one day I zoomed out and saw the part I was playing in our movie.

I didn't care for this character I created for myself.

So I ended it abruptly.

When I find myself awake at 3:00 am I wonder about our alternate endings.

How might things have been if I saw myself as a different character?

The leading lady perhaps?

Never mind ...

you treat those characters even worse.

Pain Loves Denial

If we avoid pain it doesn't go away.

It just grows

Dark sadness infesting all parts of us.

Weight of dense energy,

Collapsing down upon already aching shoulders.

Heavy on a grieving heart.

Suppressing all opportunities for joy.

Main Character

The stories I tell myself ...

Like main character energy for real

But I am the main character in my story

Which is better than being someone else's

supporting actress

The one who gave it all up to support someone they can't even trust so they stick to them like Velcro out of fear that any moment they are away their partner will betray them.

No, thank you.

I walked away. That energy is for the leftovers, not the main course.

I'm fine dining.

There is a type of guy who feeds off the women sacrificing themselves to be the supporting actresses.

The villain of every story has a minion or more supporting their illusions for a small chance to be featured in their main events.

Carrot meets string and they are the horse chasing it.

Crumbs

Bits and pieces

As if the support will give you loyalty points that will save you from the all-too-frequent betrayals.

I write my own stories. I create my own reality. I'm the main character and I attract main characters. The difference between a main character and a villain is the villain is weak at its core. It depends on others to supply and support them, usually through manipulation or some kind of abuse.

The main characters stand on their own. Full of love. And match with others playing the same role.

But if your core isn't healed, main character energy feels too much, too good ...

I'm deserving of all the good.

It's sad she doesn't believe that for herself

and stays with you.

How To Eliminate Hate

If bigots, racists, homophobes, and misogynists shout hate
into the crowd

and no one responds,

do they even exist?

Let them scream into their hateful void without the
validation they so desperately seek.

At the heart of their existence is fear and sadness trembling
at the thought of change.

Change anyway.

Live your truth.

Our validity isn't dependent upon us defending our truth to
people committed to dogmatic hate.

Floating

Now the energy shifts.

Pain and sadness can only have a home in me

If I want them to stay

I tell them

It's time to go

You taught me enough

I'm ready to know love now

Feel peace

I choose floating over barely treading water

Dropping Shoes

If your grip is tight, love can't flow where it needs to be.

Spirit gets cut off by your fears.

Letting go is faith in God, your Creator,

Divine Intelligence.

Letting go lets in what you need to heal.

Gripping, clinging, and fearing will have you waiting for the next shoe to drop while love provides so many shoes that when one drops, another is quickly replaced.

But only when you let go and make room.

White People Trauma

I have white people trauma

There are the obvious ones

The loud ones

The stand don't kneel ones

The go back to your country ones

Who wish I were never born

Then there are the subtle ones

The covert ones

The ones I think are friends or family

But really aren't

They say I'm for you

But to their white peers

They say otherwise

They vote otherwise

They don't know what the big deal is

Why is everything about race with you

Just get over it

I'm not my ancestors ones

It was a long time ago ones

These ones hurt the most

They say they see me

But they don't

Truthfully

They don't really see themselves

So they can't see me

And if they can't locate their soul

How can they be an ally to mine?

These ones scare me the most.

Unsafe Water Requires Food

Unsafe water requires food

Some of us are afraid of water

Because we hear the cries of terror

They drowned in the Atlantic

Some of us eat more than we need

Not because we are gluttonous

But because we need to feel the weight

Of our body in an unknown land

Even though centuries have passed

We still aren't safe here

A Cursed Dream

This dream is a nightmare

The land you stole is cursed

Everything you build here will crumble

May not be in this lifetime

But eventually

You can't own

What was never yours, to begin with

And the lengths you went to

To claim it

Will haunt you in unimaginable ways

Not because I wish that upon you

But energy has a way of balancing itself out

You can't purposefully

Move the scales in your favor

And not expect momentum to snap back

That's physics

The Stake in Your Eye

I don't know if you can repair

The damage done by your ancestors

Without first healing what it was in them

That made them do it

And what it is in you

That has allowed you to perpetuate it.

Do you mean perpetuate it

And benefit from it?

Because you do

Generations to Come ...

Dear colonizer

Was it worth it?

When you killed us

You killed parts of yourself

When you enslaved us

You made yourself a slave

Your generations carry the sins

Of your transgressions, until they decide

No more

And they heal what was in your DNA

That made you kill that way

So they can repair

The destruction

Created

By

Your

Greed

Ego

Soulless

Self

No Freedom Here

I used to be jealous of you. I used to watch you move easily through life. Free. Accepted. You fit in where I didn't. I thought maybe if I straightened my hair, I'd be more accepted. But I hated straight hair on me. I looked like an imposter. I thought if you could just get to know me, you'd see how amazing I am. Then we became friends. I saw how you interacted with brazen disrespect to your parents not always to their face but in the way you lied to them without blinking. I discovered how careless you were with your bodies, the drugs you sniff up your nose, the excessive dieting, the self-abuse, the alcohol consumption . . .

And sure, black people did those things too, but we were struggling, we were in pain, we were (are) oppressed, so we "used" to escape.

Why did you use it? What were you escaping from? Your people created this colonized world, so why escape? Then it dawned on me, you are less free than me, and deep down, you know it. Sure, maybe you have some privileges, but your privileges come at a cost. Your freedom comes at the price of my ancestors. You appeared free only because of how you and yours oppressed me and mine. And when I realized that, I saw right through the facade of the privilege I thought you had. Cuz freedom built on the backs of others is a link in the chain of your own oppressed mind. You can't free yourself, so you make sure others aren't free too. But see, that's where you have betrayed yourself. I found freedom not conforming to your world. The freedom I have within me isn't because I have oppressed someone else, it's because I have shifted into love and where there is love, there is freedom. We both know what we do to others we

76

also do to ourselves. I see the oppressive games you play to maintain your fragile idea of freedom, and you know I see it, and it bothers you that I am not jealous anymore, because your whole identity rests squarely upon my oppression and the idea of me believing I am oppressed.

And so, as I set myself free, where does that leave you? That's the question you need to ask yourself. That's where your healing begins.

Who are you if you are no longer privileged? That's why you fear us so much. Our liberation threatens your privileged identity.

No Love and No Light

Don't patronize me. Don't cheer me on in my healing if you aren't doing your inner work of decolonization. Your ancestors are at the center of colonization. You have deep healing work, too. My ancestors suffered abuse, your ancestors inflicted it. The abuser's energy is packed deep with self-hate and self-violence. How's your self-talk? Do you love yourself?

I know you tried to love and light your way out of this work with positive vibes, but your energy speaks the truth to your performative activism. I can tell the who are ones doing their decolonizing work and the ones who aren't. Energy is everything. Performance vs. authenticity

I've learned to navigate this white-centered world by reading energy ... who is emotionally safe for me, who only tolerates me, who doesn't see me as black (this isn't a good thing), and who pretends to care but really doesn't. The ones that care because it looks bad if they act like they don't.

I'm not angry, even though the tone of this letter might appear to be so to you. I'm just matter-of-factly no longer sparing your feelings and protecting you from feeling uncomfortable from the burdens and curses of oppressing others you knowingly or unknowingly have benefited from. You might feel some guilt. How you deal with that guilt will define you. Are you going to heal from it or bypass it to another generation and burden them with your lack of courage?

Oppression fatigue is real, and I have two choices—roll over and go to sleep or reclaim my energy and the energy of my ancestors to help people heal from the disease of colonialism from which we all suffer.

Truth be told, those who are suffering the most are the ones working overtime to pretend it doesn't exist. The oppressor is always the most tormented. "But I'm not doing it?" If you are not actively doing something to dismantle it, then yes, you're doing it.

Yt folx must be exhausted trying to breathe stolen breath. Don't you know you have lungs of your own? You can use those lungs for healing instead of denying and stealing.

Oppressors hate it when you speak of freedom for all because they have to acknowledge the part they played in oppression and how it destroys the soul from within. To speak of Jesus and uphold oppressive systems is a dark lie.

At the root of it all is a lack of self-love. Shining light on the truth illuminates and dismantles internalized oppression. It clears it. So then love can flood into those spaces and heal us all.

This denial of truth is a denial of love because love only exists in truth. To be absent of truth is to be absent of Love. Love is the only way through.

The Words That Liberated Me

Small Revolutions

How does changing the world sound today?

Not the entire world

Just yours

Not a revolution

But an evolution

A daily acceptance of self

Mixed with a commitment

To shift deeper into love

And further from fear

A slow-moving shift

Only you can feel within

Yet on the outside

Appears sudden

We think that

"She changed overnight?"

"Everything happened all of a sudden!"

But we know it's never that way

We know what needs to change

And once we acknowledge it

There's no escape

When the unknown becomes known

It's unavoidable

We might resist

However, momentum has other plans

The choice

Ride the waves of the change

Or drown in our resistance to it

I'm changing

Flowing

Riding these waves

This has been a continuous shift

Stagnant energy is suffocating

And I prefer to breathe

Grace

I'm creating space for forgiveness

As a daily practice

For the reclamation of my soul

Because in forgiveness

There is presence

Gratitude

Appreciation

But my anger needs to be acknowledged

Felt

Heard

Not compartmentalized

Or bypassed

It's little me not understanding how

People can be so cruel

It's big me confused by

Lack of consciousness

And that's it

I forgive the unconscious

They are blind to their pain

And the pain they perpetuate

They don't know love

So they cause hurt

Project anger

And that gets flung in my direction

Get off, you parasite

Eating me from inside

Rest

It's time to be in a space where resistance is no longer a mainstay.

We once believed we had to fight to make sure they didn't come for us.

But now they are coming for themselves.

All we need to do is rest while the destruction plays out.

Fill Yours First

Your purpose is to be and live your truth. To design a life that you don't have to escape or numb from. To be in the right relationship with yourself, your soul, the people you surround yourself with, and the Earth. Without this alignment, everything will feel fleeting and empty. In order to find this alignment, seek to fill yourself with love and grace. Pour love into your heart and allow that energy to spill into every aspect of your life.

Do not attempt to give to others from your well. Instead, pour so much into yourself that your love overflows and spills onto others like healing rain.

Evaporation

My peace comes from love
It makes the shadows fade

My Juice

I'm here to be wild and free, juicy and emotional.

I fall into the depths of pleasure and rebirth myself with every cry and moan I feel and release from my body.

If there is pain I will scream as to not have it become buried as a cancerous resentment in my body that poisons souls. I love being human, full of expressive contradictions and synchronicities.

Magic.

It's why we are here.

To feel, to be, to create, to be free.

So This Is Love

You really must love me

I haven't been my best

but you don't see it that way

You see it as a test

A level of intimacy

You really must love me

My hair isn't always done

My legs aren't smooth

Raw and real

I can just be

You really must love me

I always push you away

You thought it best not to chase

You didn't want me to stray

Yet you set me free

You must really love me

I sparkle in your eyes

You can't get enough

You're always hungry

Devour me

Mirroring

What you say to another you say to yourself.

What you believe about another you believe about yourself.

The shame you spew is the shame within you.

The love you speak is the love you feel within you.

Don't be surprised when the world reflects this back to you.

Goddess

Women have the power to create worlds.

Many men who are jealous of the womb seek to control it.

Women who have handed their power over to men have lost control of their wombs.

But the womb is God and will prevail despite false deities and oppressive systems.

God cannot be controlled by man.

God seeks wild.

God rules freedom.

God has the power to create or destroy as it feels necessary.

So does a woman.

God is a woman.

Only Believe in Love

We could save ourselves time and energy if we stopped believing the oppressor held the keys to our liberation. Convincing the ones who believe we shouldn't exist that we have the right to exist isn't the final step of freedom. The embodiment of our liberation is the master key to living freely. As long as we spend our days disappointed, in fear of, arguing with, and in pain over those who fight against our existence, we will never be free. Paradoxically, those in fear of love and freedom will always exist. Live as if their opinions don't matter. It's when we acknowledge their voice, that they pull energy from us to use against us. And we then drop into fear and fight with them. That's how they take our liberties from us. We believe that the structures and laws are more powerful than our souls. They are not. We must live with the understanding that universal laws are most aligned in love. Hating or fearing the other does not bring favor or fortune. Those that hate are suffering. Love energy drives those attached to this world mad. While they are literally trapped in their madness, you must continue to liberate yourself despite them. Freedom begins within, despite what the world tells you.

Depth

I loved you at the cellular level. The soul level. I wasn't caught up in your appearance, but appearances are what defined you. You weren't really for me in the way I thought you were. But I discovered that I was for me in this process and I embodied this soul-level love for myself.

In your rejection of me, I accepted myself.

The truth is, it was a blessing.

Not even a rejection.

Thank you.

Commitments

You know how I know you loved me more than her.

You chose her to abuse and set me free.

Or maybe that's too catty.

I loved myself enough to accept the truth of who you are
and she believed that commitment lied in making you
prove your love for her was real.

How frustrating for her to chase love in that way.

She wanted your commitment never committing to herself.

Gray

I didn't mean to fall in love.

I didn't mean for it to be with you.

I dreamed of loving like this,

Falling

Deep into the abyss ...

I have to surrender now.

It takes too much energy

To suppress and fight.

I can't care anymore

If it's wrong or right ...

It just is.

We just are.

It's not so black or white.

It's not easy or sure

But between us

It's clear

It's pure

There is gravity between us

We try to fight

We pull

We resist

But it's pointless

I can't get away from your

Touch ... or your

taste ... or your

Sound ... your voice haunts me

you resonate through me

inhabiting my body ...

you carefully built your heart inside of mine

now I can't live without you

Cycles

I know what you're doing

Getting yourself in control

Believing it's nothing

That you can do both

But the truth is you know

You know

How much energy it takes

To resist this love

Drained

Distracted

She won't do

But you won't give in

Until

Until it's too much

Fast asleep

You wake

Texting me

Before you know it

Pressing send

Why do you resist

What's the point

We always come back

And you remember

Why

You

Can't

Let

Go

Memories come back

No longer suppressed

My breath

My sound

My taste

My touch

It's the best

And that scares you

I'm scared too

You are my best

My favorite

My soul

No matter what you do

Where you go

I'm there

And you're here.

Boundless Love

He traced a heart with his fingertips into her palm. The sensation sent goosebumps up her arm. She shivered. A lost smile briefly found its way back to her lips.

"I love your smile." Briel's breath was staccato. He still managed to smile.

"Shhhh. Save your energy." Tears pooled in Kayla's eyes. Her smile fell just enough for Briel to notice.

"Don't stop. I want it to be the last thing ..."

"No. Please stop talking," Kayla pleaded. She willed the corners of her mouth to curl, but the dam of tears broke onto her cheeks. Droplets fell to their hands.

"Kayla ... You should know, it's always been you. I've always loved ..."

"Why do you insist on talking now? You need to save your breath. The Realm is collapsing. Your life force energy is all you have until the grid recharges." Kayla furiously scrubbed away at tears. She couldn't wipe them fast enough. "I can't lose you, again."

"No matter what, Kayla, I'm here."

"Not if you're dead."

Darkness covered her before a bright green light illuminated the room.

"Simulation complete," echoed through her head.

Kayla curled into her body. Bawling.

"Why can't you change this?" she screamed. "It's a simulation, so change the data!"

Her screams trailed into oblivion. No one answered. Flat anger consumed her tears.

"This must be hell. Same thing. Over and over. This. Is. Hell."

A microphone thumped. Speaker static crackled in her ears. An automated voice filled in.

"This is your program."

"I'm depressingly aware. Thanks."

"You're welcome."

"Sarcasm! What kind of AI are you that you don't get sarcasm?"

"The changes you seek lie within your heart."

Kayla's words cut in, "My heart is broken. He's gone."

"You can try again tomorrow," the AI plainly stated.

"Torture. No thanks." Kayla pulled herself up to stand. The green light dimmed. She grabbed her oxygen helmet and pressed the exit button. Fiery orange light burned the sky. She clicked her helmet in place and stepped into the dust.

The ground crackled under her feet. Nothing but dust particles filled the space that was once the Pacific Ocean. Or what was thought to have been an ocean. After The Realm collapsed two years ago, the only possible way to see the remnants of the earth was through simulations. Yet, even then, it was all a simulation; we just didn't realize it. Nothing was real. Kayla and the rest of the world were struck by this unfortunate truth after the Realm Grid became infected with an alien-coded virus. No human being on the planet could clear away this virus that exposed everything for what it was—a simulation. But once the virus spread throughout 95 percent of the Realm Grid, reality, as Kayla knew it, collapsed. Included in the destruction was Briel.

"Friends since babes" is how Kayla's mom described her friendship with Briel. Inseparable. Not lovers though. Kayla wasn't ready to see her best friend as a possible lover. She believed she'd be ready someday. She wanted to finish her required operations training first, and then she would tell him. She even had a dress picked out. The Realm virus made sure her someday never came. Now he was gone and even in the simulation, she couldn't bring herself to hear Briel say he loves her. He was half Borge, and no entity with Borge parts survived.

Her memory slipped into the pre-virus past.

"You are real to me. More real than any of these lame-os," Kayla snarked in the classroom. A few heads turned. She was unbothered.

"I feel more real, too." Briel smiled at her. She helplessly returned the sentiment.

"I love your smile, Kayla."

"Goodness, you're such a dork!" She always avoided the intimacy she craved.

In a perfect robotic British accent, Briel played intimacy hot potato to help Kayla save face. "Borge to you, young fem human. Only humans are dorks. I, Briel the Borge, am incapable of dorkness." They crumbled in their perfect for one another laughter.

The ground crumbled into bits. Dry rock pieces and dust shuffled beneath her feet. Kayla approached the front door. She lifted her hand over a security palm reader. The door lifted open. She shoveled herself in. The door slammed shut behind her. The oxygen helmet came off. She inhaled deep. Her tension kept her from remembering to exhale completely. Kayla lifted the case covering the house grid. "OFFLINE" blinked. She pressed a green button.

"Limited simulations available until further notice," an automated voice said into the quiet space. Some lights turned on. Other lights flickered. A dog barked, excited for her arrival, and scrambled toward her, but stopped short of an actual greeting when the scene replayed itself over and over.

"I wish I could pet you too, Jasper," Kayla quietly affirmed.

Kayla turned on her shower. Steam encapsulated the bathroom. The mirror fogged up. Wrapped in her towel, she allowed her heart to lead her fingertip. Against the mirror, she cut through the fog. "I love you too." Kayla stepped back. Through the etched parts, she saw her reflection broken into tiny pieces within the letters. A reflected light flickered in the "Y." Kayla squinted closer into the mirror. Silver light flickered again. She followed the trail of the reflection to the shelf behind her. Her eyes pulled her closer. Silver particles danced and came together. In a trance, she studied the particles pulling and shaping themselves in a silver necklace. At the center of the necklace, the particles organized into a heart-shaped locket. Kayla blinked and readjusted her focus. The silver particles settled into a solid form.

"How?" she whispered.

"Energy is everything," the AI robot voice whispered in return.

"I—I guess it is ..."

Kayla snatched the locket and turned the shower off.

Back in the simulation room, Kayla switched on the green light.

"Simulation starting. Please select your program."

Kayla turned away from the touch screen. Closing her eyes, she held the heart-shaped locket close to her heart. She exhaled long and wide.

The green screen filled in. Briel stood beside her.

"Open your eyes."

Kayla gasped at Briel's voice, not trusting to open her eyes out of disbelief.

"Open your eyes," Briel repeated.

Kayla gently peeked. Then exhaled to completion. He was there. A new simulation.

"How did you bring up this new simulation?" Briel asked.

Kayla smiled, "I followed my heart."

On Purpose

1. The hypercritical voices in your head don't ever go away because this world is noisy. Instead, fall deeply in love with yourself. With deep self-love, the critical voices get muffled and harder to hear. They lose their power. And without power, they lose creditability. The goal is to believe and increase the love voices and to quiet the anxious voices. Do not waste your energy resisting the voices. Just say "I love you" over and over until that's the only voice you hear.
2. Self-love is where we plant seeds for change. Seeds of love we plant within our hearts that one by one grow a forest of healing that nourishes the planet.

Soul Speaks

I listen. I listen because there was a time I didn't. Times
when I chose deafness to remain safe and comfortable from
my truth. Times when I felt my life force slipping away
moment by moment because I didn't want to do the
uncomfortable, overwhelming work of listening. Because
to listen is to tune out of the programming you were taught
you must follow to make it in this world. To listen means
others will not listen to you. Not only will they turn away
from you, but they will also talk about you, shame you, and
discredit you. They will do this because your listening
reminds them they are choosing silence over their soul.
And they KNOW this isn't right. They FEEL their soul
dying. They HEAR their soul screaming, but they turn their
backs on themselves in a twisted self-betrayal sickness that
forces them to numb themselves with vices they justify as
fun. Because listening to their souls' voices means they will
have to admit they have been lying. Lying to themselves
and others about their truth. I decided listening was the
only way to live in a world of people dying from silencing
themselves in fear of the unknown. There is so much
freedom here because I can hear myself. I can feel what's
real. There is nothing to prove. It feels like absolute
resolve. I am forever supported in this upside-down world
of silence. I can hear the connection where they chose the
quiet. The valley to this promised land was wrought with
battles, and I fought the illusions. I feared if I saw the truth,
would I even like what I saw? But a voice kept telling me,
anything is better than a lie. When you live a lie, you never
feel safe because you know it's not supported without more
lies, and lies drain and deplete you worse than the most

dangerous drug. So, I listened, I battled, and won the war for truth.

The only uncomfortable part now is seeing where others don't live their truth ...

When you remove the veil, you see all the lies people live. But it's not my place to save them. Only they can save themselves. However, when another awakens, we recognize the light of truth in the other and we spill tears for the other in celebration.

We say, "You made it through!" because we both know what we had to go through to get *here*.

It's a beautiful story of self-love and grace to align with all that is and ever was.

Cherish Me

Cherish me with actions that match your energy

If moments contradict,

Then Cherish me with truth

And unquestionable integrity.

Cherish me with kindness

I'll naturally return the favor

Let grace lead us into

Higher vibrations together

Cherish me with our words of love

Fill me with pleasure

Hold it down

I will crown you a master

A king

Me your queen

We can rule this life together

A united front

Forever and ever

As Within

Her reflection pierced deep.

The mirror restored her sense of being.

She could see herself. Finally.

No judgment

No competition

No conditions

Acceptance. Finally.

Her beauty

Her worth

Connected only to her soul

She felt herself from within

A Quick Word About Boundaries

Boundaries are the handbook to your soul. They teach others how to show up for you. Boundaries reveal where you support yourself and where you abandon your needs.

We also don't realize that a lack of boundaries shows up in our bodies in ways we would never suspect. The physical manifestation of inconsistent boundaries can surface as autoimmune diseases, digestive problems, inflammation, and a general imbalance in our nervous system in the form of unbalanced hormones, metabolism, and mood.

Boundaries are not limited to words expressed, telling someone what you do or don't like. Boundaries are your internal energy supported by the action you take. So you can see why it's so super important you stay committed to self-love.

Circumstances do not have a mind of their own..

The slides of reality cannot independently pick and choose what you experience.

That is a fundamental impossibility.

You are the consciousness that attracts or draws in every single slide of reality that you experience through your vibration—which is generated through your daily thoughts and beliefs.

What you think about all day long (or lack of it) is what you manifest. Your mental chatter is what draws in your everyday experiences.

You cannot manifest something new by allowing your thoughts to run wild all day long. "Doing the affirmations" and then spending the rest of the day thinking about the lack of your desire regurgitates the lack—it invites the absence back in because you keep retelling yourself the same story.

When you sit down and focus your affirmations and you get inundated with happiness and bliss, those feelings mean that it is on its way to you. The FEELING is the manifestation! Instead of crashing back down, stay in the feeling. Stay in the vibration. Watch how FAST (I've seen it occur in minutes) your manifestation, even just the beginning stages, finds you!

More Cycles

I don't think you realize the effect your soul has on mine. You wander around this earth, running from this job to the next, working and working, but you're really just avoiding life and avoiding me.

Don't you see you're running from me? From us? You try so hard to keep yourself from giving in to this love your soul needs, but your head keeps saying no ... No, your feelings aren't real. You tell yourself this isn't practical and will hurt too many people, or others will be angry if you admitted that it was me all along. Seventeen years later, you still can't get me out of your head. You still think about me every day, reliving memories of us wishing you could just feel me today. I know you struggle with your feelings because I feel what you feel.

You can't get away from me. I can't get away from you. We share the same soul. The pain would dissipate if we just accepted this instead of fighting it.

What I Know

I know you

I know your voice

your whisper

your sound

I know you

I know your body

each valley

each peak

I know you

I know your heart

your rhythm

your rhyme

I know you

I know your thoughts

I read your heart

I speak speak your poetry

I know you

I know your love

Your touch

Your taste

I can't wait

The anticipation is intense

More than I expected
knowing you so well
hasn't calmed the excitement
of living life with you

WTF

Who are you

And

Why do you keep showing up?

I don't think

I

Like you very much

Not knowing you

But

You come off as self-involved

Yet the moments

Of

Our chance meetings make me think

Who are you

And

Why do you keep showing up?

Not my type

At

All, but you keep tryin'

You are silly

Or

You are good at faking

I'm too strong

For

Games you like to play

Yet the moments

Of

Our chance meetings make me think

Who are you

And

Why do you keep showing up?

Seek Change

The first mistake is believing in sameness.

Same thinking.

Same feeling.

Same seeing.

Same hearing.

Same experiencing.

Difference and chance are what are most consistent.
Consistently inconsistent is the sweet spot.

Variety and diversity are divinity.

Sameness is stuckness in the oppression of depression.
Change creates liberation.

The birdsong continues even when it rains.

So should you.

Where's Heaven?

Heaven is when we realize happiness and joy is abundant to us right now while we are living on Earth.

Hell is for those who judge the ones living unapologetically happy and joyous.

Y'all are miserable and it shows.

Too Far From Water

Sitting with the discomfort in a desert that drained me dry. It's not the desert's fault. It's no one's fault. Rather a fire of souls that burned one another to ashes. In my thirst for life, I buried my ashes at the bottom of the sea. The volcano erupted from the depths of my ocean and gave rise to something beautiful in me.

Magic Words

Words are symbols of magic. When combined in certain ways they carry vibrational messages to the Universe. Those messages shape our experiences. Speak words you want to experience in life. Speak your experiences into words.

"You were exactly what needed to happen for me in the time that it happened."

For me ... not to me ... it was **for** me.

Faith

It's crazy how hurt I felt then compared to how free I feel now. I hope the same thing for you and for anyone who has ever felt so devastatingly crushed by something that you can't see the light or the tunnel.

Just pitch black.

But when you let go and sit in the void and trust beyond what you can't see in front of you, and you take steps forward anyway, life falls into a precious order.

It all comes together so beautifully that you believe that magic, God, Source, The Universe, angels, guides . . . all of It is one and It is all working for YOU.

We are so supported and so loved.

This life is amazing when you zoom out and hold space for it with love.

Have faith.

Nourishment

When I was a little girl, my mom put me on a liquid-fast diet just in case so I wouldn't get fat.

My dad told me no man really likes chubby girls. I watched my parents constantly talk about their weight, other people's bodies, and mine obsessively.

I wanted to disappear.

So starving myself could help me accomplish not being seen. Cuz if they couldn't SEE me then they, my parents and whoever, couldn't abuse me.

Except my body couldn't get thin enough, fast enough, and my boobs just kept growing.

And my boobs brought all kinds of attention to me. My dad was wrong. The boys liked my body and my boobs . . .

a little too much.

I was basically a body with big tits and not too many guys could see past that.

So I made them smaller.

I was shrinking again.

I got as small as my body would allow which wasn't small enough, and the boys still wouldn't leave me alone.

At one point I used it to empower myself over them. It was the only way I could find power at the time. I hated that though.

I just wanted my body to look a certain way so I could love it. Feel comfortable in it.

But it's always, "believe it before you see it."

As within, so without

So I just started believing it.

And slowly seeing it.

I don't know if others saw a difference, but I felt a difference and that was all that mattered.

Taking Space

The old habits of wanting to disappear linger sometimes, but instead of starving myself, I push myself forward to be seen. To feel my love.

I'm thirsty.

Not for others to notice me, but for myself to feel comfortable being noticed and not care about how they notice me or why they do.

The only thing that matters is I notice me, I feel me, I protect me, I have grace for me, I love me.

Unconditionally.

Self-love is an act of rebellion in a society that compartmentalizes worth into conformity boxes.

I love my life outside the box.

I love me.

Beacon

What you're clinging to is also what is holding you back.

Let go.

And after you let go, you have to deconstruct your energy, release parts that produce or attract pain, and then rebuild yourself to become a beacon of bliss and love.

And the hardest part is trusting the goodness of it all. Believing you deserve the best and no longer settling for crumbs to survive on.

You have to want your wholeness more than the comfort of old habits and outdated beliefs.

You have to care about how you feel.

Forward

Every word I express is a forward movement into healing. A reflection on the past is just that, a reflection.

Something I zoom out on and examine so I can find healing truth in it.

Sometimes I have to slice through my pain with my tongue to taste the sweetness of my own resilience.

Or use a pen to dice up the shame in my shadow, rearrange her parts, to empower her every move.

All The Words That Heal Me

Words that churn my gut

To spill out as cathartic liberation

Words that were secrets kept

To protect the betrayers

Words that replayed movies

Of a life lived

Stories of naive hope

Hope

The way the sun rises

After darkness

All the words that heal me.

You broke me open but you didn't break me.

You showed me where I was wrong about myself.

The parts of me I thought were unlovable.

I thought I needed you to love me.

But it's impossible to ask a man to do a woman's job.

I explored the womb of my soul and found my own pleasure to create within.

My faulty program needed you to torture me into releasing my suffering.

When I set myself free, I grew wings that flew over every lie you told.

I became new.

Butterfly

I set myself free when I got honest with myself.

Then ...

I set my mother free.

I set my daughter free.

I set my sons free.

I set my husband free.

Liberated people liberate others.

All The Words That Love Me

Plenty Of Room

I take up space.

Lots of it.

Big boob, magic pussy, energy, and everything I touch levels up or shrinks depending upon your ability to embody your magnificence.

There's enough room for us all to take up the space we need.

I'm here to spread love and pollinate the universe with bliss.

What's your purpose?

Trust This

What we want, wants us back.

What we love, loves us back.

When we don't trust, we cling.

When we cling we expect what we cling to

to prove itself trustworthy.

But that never works.

Let go and see where the energy falls into place.

Trust your intuition above all else.

Love is liberating.

Always.

This is what I wanted

Love that stands the test of time

Love that faces hard truths

Love that comes back stronger than before

Love that holds my heart carefully

And a fierceness that melts into bliss

Love that has inside jokes

Silliness

Authenticity

And let me remind you of your worth

Love that says "You got this"

"I got you"

"Let's figure this out"

"I love it when you smile"

"You're beautiful"

And "I can't keep my hands off you"

Love that is lazy days of sunshine

And sunset ocean swims

Doing nothing together feels like the best of everything,
kind of love

A liberation in trust kind of love

This is the kind of love I wanted

This is the love I have

—the love I always wanted was right in front of me

Thirsty

I'm thirsty for my own energy

Not yours

See society tried to program me before I bled

Men groped and fondled me before I was ten

My sexual agency was stolen from me

Shamed into me

And I didn't have a choice

Then

But now I do

I choose to reclaim my pleasure

My sensual nature

And I display it as I see fit

Cuz that's how I reclaim it

You have no say in the matter

And if you do, then I will know you have yet to reclaim yourself and probably live in fear of your sex

I'm liberating you when I liberate myself but you find judgment in that

Someone has to go first on the path to freedom.

I'll go whether or not you come, but I know as I take these steps of liberation others will break cycles with me and we will all be free to be exactly as we please.

Divine Feminine

Capable of creating and coming undone in multiple contractions of pain and pleasure no man could bear as the bearer of darkness and container of light.

This is a woman.

She bleeds with the moon

Sheds layers of creation with each cycle

Magic womb power

God lives in her veins as

a divine vessel of physical manifestation.

The Creator Is a Woman

Undeniable magic is born from her lips

And those lips

Round hips

Straight hips

It doesn't matter

The woman is God in the flesh

That's why she is a threat

To those who fear her greatness

She can do what no man has done

And will never be able to do

So weak men oppress her

Strong men praise her

Confused women deny themselves their own juice and justice because they do not know

The power that is in them

But those who embody the TRUTH carry the torch for all women, of all kinds, with and without wombs, for a Woman is what we all come from and what is within us all.

God

Goddess

Siren

Source

Creator

That is Woman.

This Part

OK, so this is the faith part ...

The ... I'm not feeling OK, second-guessing everything, but, clinging to a thread of trust, part.

The contrast, the collapse of the energy to create the new, part.

The quiet understanding, I'm going to be more than OK, part.

The ugh, this doesn't feel so good right now path to everything is working in my favor, part.

The ... I have to trust my guidance above and beyond anything else, part.

The hold on, big shifts are coming in,

part.

The ... I got "this" part.

No

You don't have to have a reason to not do the things that feel out of alignment for you.

"No" is enough of an explanation.

Does My Love of Self Threaten You?

Do you sit in judgment of how I express my body freely and wonder why I have to "do that"?

Does the softness of my curves scream I love sex and you cringe because you have shame around pleasure?

Do my incessant bikini pictures have you wondering why is that necessary?

If you have these questions or something similar, I can tell you I take pics of myself because I used to judge other women who did it ... until I realized my judgment was a projection of my own limitations and disconnections.

I was resentful because they felt free in their bodies and I didn't.

But I longed for my own liberation.

I understood only I had the power to set myself free.

So I did.

And I have zero regrets. I love my body. I love feeling sexy. I love embodying my liberation and expressing myself however I want. I recommend we all free ourselves from the shackles and from an oppressive culture that shames sex and perverts it into people who end up secretly cheating and hiding their porn addictions ... or worse ...

all rooted in unhealed sexual trauma.

Posting pics I love of myself is how I reclaim my energy from those who took it from me against my will.

When I allowed myself to soften my body, and soften my energy, I created more room for love and abundance to flow to and from me, raising my overall vibration.

Energy flows best through grounded/open circuits.

Kind vs. Nice

Fuck being a nice girl.

I'm kind, but I'm not "nice." I don't care for nice.

Nice feels like passive-aggressive manipulation. "I'm nice so you have to be nice too." But it feels fake because that niceness is a tactic to get something or has expectations attached to it.

Or it's pretending.

"I'm acting as if it doesn't bother me but it does" niceness.

Niceness is spiritual bypassing.

Nice doesn't feel all their feelings.

Kindness feels like authenticity to me.

It's real, not a show.

Not an effort to people please.

Kindness says, I have filled my own cup and I have something to share.

Kindness has boundaries and won't pretend everything is OK when it's not.

Kindness honors the soul.

Niceness feels like self-betrayal. You broke me open but you didn't break me.

My Flowers

To feel, to be, to create, to be free.

My love is like the sweetest kiss and the most intense sex. My orgasms are instantaneous not because he has a special skill but because I know it's safe for me to fully be in my body with him. That feeling of peace and bliss is the ultimate blessing. Sometimes I question how deserving I am because of my past. But he reminds me we all have a past.

When flowers lose their petals in the winter does that mean they don't deserve to bloom again?

Spring answers that question.

So bloom.

Medicine

The medicine you seek is you.

Not him.

Not her.

Not them.

You.

You know what you need to do.

Now do it.

Automagically

Everything happens for me *automagically*.
Do you believe?

.

It's not supposed to make sense to anyone else.

It just hast to be true for you.

Stick With It

Right when you feel like giving up is when everything starts falling into place. Keep going. The seed is just about to burst into the light.

Nothing to Prove

You have nothing to prove.

It's already yours.

And if you have to prove it to someone,

Prove it to yourself.

You are the only one that can truly appreciate your journey.

Because no one has lived your life but you.

The Spectrum

Everything exists on a spectrum ...

So if it was toxic, it could also be beautiful. The love that broke your heart also taught you how to love and heal yourself. The story we tell ourselves after it ends or after we let go is the story we carry with us into the next chapter.

Love cleans the slate.

Love clears the energy.

Love raises the vibration.

True love heals all.

Unconditionally.

Forever.

My Part

I wish you the best

The pain you triggered within me needed to surface

Thank you for revealing to me what needed healing in me.

I'm sorry if I hurt you

I'm sorry for being drama when you needed peace

I'm sorry

Please forgive me

Thank you

I love you

Clearing the energy

Releasing it

I hope you are well.

I love you.

Moon Girl

like the phases of the moon

she knew her darkness

was just part of the process

that lit her fire

and made the angels sing

There

She

Glows

Change

Every phase of her life

Wrecked her

Healed her

Transformed her

Gave birth to her

She faced everything head on

As her soul commanded

Crashing into her limitations

A meteorite busting atmospheres

Setting fire to herself

Rising through the ashes

She welcomed change

This too shall pass ...

Anxiety makes you see think things that aren't real. You think they are talking about you. You think he doesn't really love you. You think it's all going to end, whatever "it" is, because you laughed at the wrong time or cried or stayed quiet or whatever, it doesn't matter. You just know you did it wrong and now everything is ruined because of it. So, to stay safe from destroying everything around you, you stay hidden, guarded, fake, anything you can to stay protected. But that is so lonely of you. It's not always this bad, but some days it just is. Then, you find that one person to talk to. The one who understands. And together you find the ground, plant your feet, and the fog of it all clears again.

Loving Me

I love you, but I struggle with loving myself so I've been working really hard to heal all the traumas in my life because someone once said you can only love someone as much as you love yourself. And man do I want you to have the best parts of me, so in these few years I have faced my darkest demons all in the name of love.

I love me.

I never knew I could be so brave.

But here I am, loving myself despite what the trauma says.

Just the way God intended.

To not be of the world.

But to be about God's love.

That's self-love.

God

But I don't think we'll lose contact for too long, because, like a beacon, I'm always being called to you.

God is always there.

Real Life Love

Some days my anxiety and insecurities get the best of me and I'm afraid you'll stop loving me.

However, you are here with me. You show up in the best ways even if it's the smallest way and I love that about you Even if at first I may say it's not enough.

God, you are enough.

Everything you are is enough and I thank God for every single second with you.

You taught me how to love myself.

It's Me Not You

There's nothing you can do that can stop me from loving you. Nothing. And I pray you know any time I've acted in the most unloving ways toward you is when I didn't love myself. I'm learning that the better I am at loving myself, the better I'll be at loving you.

Unexpected Blessings

Thank you for not believing in all we could be

Thank you for wearing that played-out mask and committing yourself to the same BS

Thank you for showing me what's possible without you

Thank you for never being who you said you were

Thank you for not choosing me so I can learn how to choose myself

I appreciate all you never did for me so I could see the scrub you are

You showed me all I never wanted to believe you were.

But I believe it now

And I'm thankful

Because I'm free

Gratitude

I did love you, but you brought out the worst in me. And I'm thankful for that, as those parts of me had to come out so I can see all the ways I didn't love myself. I'm not angry anymore. Instead I have gratitude because without that experience I wouldn't be who I am now.

I love myself.

Thank you.

Believe

In those moments when it feels most challenging, you are being asked to jump into the unknown and have faith. There are solutions, even though we don't see them ... but they are there, in the energy, waiting for someone to believe in the possibility of them.

Believe

Healing Ways

Sometimes we attract romantic partners who mimic past trauma.

We attract the pain that needs to be healed in us and because that pain feels familiar we mistake it for connection and love.

We know the difference because it will either make us contract, feel dense heaviness, and withdraw from the world, keeping it a secret, much like how past trauma shut us down (trauma bond).

Or it will expand us into liberation from that trauma story, encouraging us to free ourselves.

Uplifting us with peace and love that brings clarity.

Shift Solution

The solution does not exist within the same frequency or vibration as the problem.

This is why you have to shift your energy away from the problem and into the energy of a solution.

Solutions require grounded clarity.

If you don't have clarity or if you are not grounded you will stay harping within the energy of the problem.

Thereby perpetuating the problem.

Find the quiet.

Focus on appreciation.

The solutions are hidden in the joyful moments of life.

The problems aren't going away

And neither are the solutions.

Live life to the fullest.

Nonconformist

I tried on conformity

it didn't fit

knots in my throat

it was filled with silence and self-betrayal

a dull heartbeat

slow death

so it wasn't for me

life's too short to live in a program where everyone is
afraid to be different

divinity is found in diversity

Cravings

Crave your own energy

Your sovereignty

Your love

The Source God within

Your happiness

Your expression

Your healing

Your liberation

Drink

Drink from

Your heart

Your grounding

Your gratitude

Your God self within

Your alignment

Your liberation

Nothing outside of you has power over you

Unless you believe it to be so

And your anger at that comes

When people test you

Is from the distraction

To that outside of you

Purposefully confusing you

Draining you

Manipulating you

To stop believing in your peace

And to believe them in their chaos

Don't believe them

They will test you

They have been testing us for centuries

They are the opposite of love

The shadow

Come to a lower vibrational force

Come to separate you from God

Through their own wounds

I see your anger

And that's exactly what feeds their vibration

Pain feeds them

Pull your energy in

Align

Expand into solutions and possibilities

Instead of

Contracting in anger and fear

Alchemize their hate into your empowerment

Once you realize who you are

It's over for them

And beginning for you ...

Be ok with change.

It's upside down until it's right side up

Where does it begin and end?

Nothing is steady.

Energy is always moving.

You're breathing.

You heart beating.

Blood pumping.

We move even we are still.

Even when our soul leaves

Our bodies still move

To disintegrate

And return to earth

Blossoms

I ground and center

A reflection of a moment so sweet

It lingers on my tastebuds for decades

Then leaves an aftertaste of bitterness

Flash it's over

How does that happen?

Just like that

... the energy drains away

... the wind sucked out

... life force gone

Renew this ripe time to grow

A seed in dark earth

Traveling toward the light

To bloom once again

Trying to figure out a time in history when religion and "morality" weren't used to oppress people who didn't conform to social norms or looked "different."

There wasn't a time.

And the outcasts prevailed.

Thank you, Jesus.

Vulnerable Spaces

Love is my fingertips tracing your vulnerable spaces

Whispering ...

It's OK

I'm here

I've got you

I'll hold you

I love you

Listen To Your Heart

Listen to your heart ... But here's the catch

It requires stillness. Silence.

As it doesn't speak loudly.

It's a subtle, consistent knowing. Not forceful.

Just a steady stream of consciousness,

Asking for you to listen.

And to find peace within your surroundings.

If no peace exists, the heart calls on you to adjust your surroundings to experience peace so you can hear your heart speak while letting go of disturbing people, situations, or beliefs that drown out your heart song.

Anyone or anything that disrupts peace

Isn't meant to stay.

They exist to show you where you aren't listening.

When there is chaos there is misalignment.

Turn away from the noise of drama.

Tune into the bliss of your soul.

This is where love waits for you.

In confident stillness.

But if you can't be still,

You will mistake the noise for love,

That projects your pain onto others.

Karmic Love

Some people come into our lives and burn us to ashes.
Through the pain, they point us toward the stories we carry
that tell us that pain and love go hand in hand. These
relationships carry lots of heartbreak and confusion. They
are karmic. When we release ourselves from believing we
must suffer for love, we strengthen our souls, and the
karma clears. It's a powerful portal for ascension. Our
ashes become rich soil for our growth.

Come With Me

Surrender me powerful

Submit me brave

I overcome

I allow

My magic to rise

From my root to the sky

I ignite

I glow

My energy flows

Between us

It burns

Fire within me

The ashes now stardust

Our bodies burst free

Boundaries

Boundaries direct your energy where to go. Without them, your energy spills into places it's not meant to be and other people's energy spills into your space when it shouldn't. This is when you don't know what your energy feels like and you end up taking on other disruptive vibrations that can easily manipulate and drain you.

Turning Point

There are moments in your life in which something happens and you realize you will never be the same. You divide these moments as before and after THIS. This is to be expected and sometimes we claw tooth and nail to go back to before THIS because it's what we know.

This is when we are being called to change.

Either we answer the call or we spend our whole lives in resistance of the inevitable.

Answer the call.

Free Yourself

Self-love allows us to breathe into change. In fact, letting go and changing is part of love's journey. It's OK to not be the same. We aren't meant to be the same because then we'd be stuck and stagnant like an icky pond. No one wants that. It's also humbling. Sometimes we fight change because it means we have to confront parts of ourselves that we'd rather hide. Change any way. You gotta see yourself to free yourself.

The Best Kind Of Change

It's not that she didn't want him to touch her. She just knew that when he did, she'd burst into delicious streams of luminous forms of ecstatic energy uncontainable within her human form and she'd never be the same in the most glorious way and she'd never be the same again.

Physics

I speak in circles to weed through my thoughts to find the
perfect words to describe how I feel, but it never comes out
right and it's long and confusing ... but then you finally
reply with the simplest response and your words are like a
magnet, pulling all my thoughts into one cohesive feeling
and it's then I'm like you just did that thing ... you get me

Cleanse

Keeping that song on repeat until I free myself from the trigger of your memory.

Not Our Ways

Stop putting limits on the ways God speaks to you. Humans have limiting beliefs and fears. Not God. God speaks through everything. Literally everything. Stay open.

Stay present. Stay in love and grace. Trust.

The Garden

The lessons of the heart always plant seeds for forward progress. Water your soul with affirmations of sweet love and watch yourself grow into the light in which you came from.

Love is where it's at.

Self-love is a sexy vibration. It is attractive and attracts to you all the energies in the vibrational frequency of love.

Get on this vibe.

Infinity

Some things change while staying the same.

You change.

The world changes.

But my love remains.

Love is infinite.

Everything

I hate that I keep dreaming about you.

How do I set myself free from these memories?

What's left to heal?

The universe has a perfect order.

Gravity keeps us in place.

The world spins,

And I will never stop loving you.

I love the quiet of when I silence my haters.

They won't come for me because they hold no power over me. I reclaimed my energy and they scurried back into their caves. *Unfuckwithable.*

Trust the intuitive path of miracles over the logical path of needing more proof. Allow love to move you through it. Love needs no proof. It stands on its own.

When you show up, spirit shows out, no doubt about it.

Happiness Really Is A Choice

Your brain is wired for survival, not happiness. If you want to be happy, you have to choose the things that will bring you joy. You have to invest in your own energy and care about how you feel. You need to pay attention to cues of unhappiness, take risks, and make changes. It's not easy, but it's necessary if you want to be happy.

It No Longer Is

It is what it is

No

It's what it was

And it's no longer what it is

Thanking My Lucky Stars

Live by the sun and dance with the moon.

Set yourself free to be all you long to be.

I wanted to be with you,

But the stars had other plans.

And those plans are so much brighter than I realized.

Just a friendly reminder that you are doing enough.

You don't need to do anymore.

Maybe consider doing less ...

Love Never Dies

When people transition, they may be physically gone, but their soul energy lives forever. Those who have passed on are here with us. Their energy is pure and present when we close our eyes and feel into our heart. We are never alone. Their love is always surrounding us.

Dreams

Allow yourself to dream

No dreams

No desires

Are you even alive?

Are you living?

Aligning is dreaming

Seeds plant themselves here

It's where possibilities are born

It's where you become beyond the program

Where you live your life

Not theirs.

How Do I Know It's Love?

You know it's love when

You can let go and it still exists

You know it's love

Because you lead with kindness

Love is liberation

There's nothing to prove

It either is or it isn't

You know it's love

When you don't have to claim them in your bio

Love isn't ownership

Love is

It has its own legs

No manipulation

No ultimatums

Just love

Love you have within

And love that matches that vibration

Juice

Unapologetic pleasure is rebellious

The kind of pleasure not dependent upon substances

The pleasure that has you vibing in your own skin

Raw

Open

Vulnerable

Dripping with sensuous love of life

Embodied yumminess.

Blessed

Even through

The most

Dark

Moments when

All

Hope

Feels

Lost

You

Still

Manage

To

Light

Me

Up in ways

No one else can

And I'm

So blessed

To know you

The Truth Is The Light

What you desire requires you

To be honest with yourself

The angels told me

You can't stay locked up

And limited in your beliefs

Expecting to feel free

Stay present with yourself

Love yourself

When you look for others to validate you

You send your energy

And your power

Away

To someone who is just as flawed as you

Know yourself

Know your energy

And you will forever feel empowered

Forever Healing

This isn't the end of my healing

Healing never ends

It's a continuous journey of unfolding

And opening

My heart

To bear witness to my soul

Vulnerable strength

To inspire you

Embrace this journey

This is it

This is what we came here for

Prologue

What is this book about?

Remembering the love that you are. Remembering you are more than just this body. Understanding you are the receiver of energy, which you transmute in your lived experience. Realizing that cutting off your ability to receive creates an imbalance, and you become too much of "this world" and not enough of the love in which you come from.

Beautiful, but ... What do you mean by too much of "this world"?

Being too much of this world means you overidentifying with form. You forget that form is nothing but your creative energy taken shape. But when you overidentify, you forget that you are the creator of what you see. And if you don't like what you see because of your painful experiences affecting your ability to receive, then you blame others for showing you the experiences and the pain that needs to be healed. You are avoiding what needs to be done before anything else. That is: Heal, resolve, and dissolve stories you inherited from other people's pain.

So go to therapy?

That's part of it. It's a start. But it's only part of the journey. It's the beginning where you see that there are parts of you that aren't aligned with the whole of you.

Can you explain that in a different way?

Before you came into this world, you were Soul Spirit Energy. Soul Spirit Energy, SSE, exists in the infinite. At this stage of your existence, there aren't words available for you to understand more. At some point, SSE decides it wants to experience form and express love beyond itself. So then it found itself on Earth, a quiet planet, and expanded itself into different species. As each level of expansion evolved and became different life forms. The expansion grew and grew until there were humans. To put it plainly, SSE mated with itself, multiplied, separated, and multiplied more, until there were millions of species expressed as a world where SSE could experience itself in infinite ways. The interesting part is SSE keeps evolving, creating while dissolving, and in doing so learns to remember itself. And it always remembers that it's love. Or better yet peace or calm.

I don't know if it can be explained at this stage, but at some point, the human form gets in the way of SSE reception. And this usually happens with the form turns on itself. Again, not sure why it turns on itself yet, but it does and it hurts life around it. When it turns from itself, it gets it is part of SSE and love and becomes too concerned with its place in existing and forgets to exist for the pleasure of existing. Better said, it becomes too concerned with controlling and less trusting of the heart.

But isn't the heart human form?

Yes! But it beats to the rhythm of its SSE source, Soul Spirit Energy Source. And that SSE Source flows freely to everyone, but in form, humans want to control how it flows to other humans and that weakens the form. You can only control the form in which you came to. That's it. You try to use force, violence, or manipulation to get the outcomes you desire, but each time you do it results in another issue that you think you need to control.

Can you explain the term "broken heart" from Spirit's perspective?

Simply put, it is the breaking down of the protective layer you have around your heart. Over the years, humans have built fortresses around themselves literally and figuratively to keep other humans from hurting them. Then one day, you decide to let someone in or closer, and being the human they are, they did something or said something that hurt you and in essence "broke your heart."

Most of you see this as a negative thing, but it actually serves a sacred purpose if you allow it to be revealed to you. It shows you where or how you rely on other humans, in all their imperfections and trauma, to save you from your pain. Other humans can distract you from or assist you in healing, but ultimately, you and your relationship with US, SSE, God, or whatever you want to call it, is where you need to turn to for the ultimate healing. Tuning into the LOVE that is you, remembering you are LOVE and only LOVE. Everything else is an illusion. When your heart breaks, the walls come down, and you have a choice: rebuild those walls or allow the love to flow in.

Heartbreak is inevitable. You can't avoid it. It's a necessary portal for you to learn more about who you are at your core. It's the sweet space of vulnerability where your walls have no power against your true emotions. The fortress built around your heart lacks the necessary strength to defend against the truth. Your heart seeks truth the way our lungs require oxygen. You can only hold your breath for so long before you suffocate, gasping for air.

Grasping for truth. And your whole life can be the version of you grasping, or you can let go of what isn't true and breathe peacefully. You have a choice.

So this "choice" is free will?

Yes. You are so free, you can choose to suffer. You are so free, you can choose fear over love. You are so free, you can choose to believe in your oppression or believe in your liberation.

Wait. What are you saying? People are choosing their oppression?

People choose to believe the stories of the oppressor instead of the truth of their souls. But people are learning that the truth of their soul, love, has more power than any oppression story. These are the people rallying against the "-isms" of the world. They are choosing to speak their truth and live their lives regardless of any manmade laws or beliefs. Man is not the authority.

SSE is. Soul Spirit Energy is the ultimate authority. Those who trust the love of the Soul know no man has power over them no matter how much they try to exert or manipulate it over others.

This doesn't deny that systems were designed to suppress specific groups. Those systems were created by humans who overidentified with their human form and believed they held the power from God, but actually they lost sight of their connection to spirit and love. They became obsessed with control to the point that they oppressed themselves in the process.

Remember, what you do to another, you do to yourself.
You, We, are all connected!